73

*Atrophy*

 C**ʒ**

Poems by Jackson Burgess

Write Bloody Publishing
*America's Independent Press*

Los Angeles, CA

writebloody.com

Burgess, Jackson
1ˢᵗ edition.
ISBN: 978-1938912894

Cover Design by Zoe Norvell
Interior Layout by Winona Leon
Edited by Katie Hogan
Proofread by Ruth Madievsky


Type set in Bergamo from www.theleagueofmoveabletype.com

Printed in the USA

Write Bloody Publishing
Los Angeles, CA

Support Independent Presses
writebloody.com

*A*TROPHY

# ATROPHY

## I.

## II.

## III.

# IV.

# Lily

# I.

# Van Gogh
*after Richard Siken*

I take off my fingertips, send them in packing peanuts,
and though you don't want them, you toss them in the freezer
just in case I want them back. I pull out my widow's peak,
inches of hair by now you've never seen, slap on a stamp,
send it along. In the story I don't tell anyone,
my heart is a town—cottages, cobblestone, courtyard and all.
You're the butcher, carving lamb chops. Of course
I'm the town drunk. 5am again and the lamps
are sputtering to make way for day. Okay, I'm sorry
I called you the butcher. What I'm getting at
is have you ever seen a gas station
that's gone under, the nozzles draped in yellow tape,
the green plastic screens dustswept? It's no fun,
like me landing in your hometown and calculating the odds
of brushing shoulders in the terminal with someone
whose shoulder you once brushed. So I take off my shoulder
and Saran Wrap it up, tape a tight package to protect
the dust you may recognize when you slice in
with your cleaver, clear some space on the block.
I'd rather not mention the nights I spent wailing barside
with friends who were not really friends. The taps
dripped what looked like sympathy and I'm ashamed to say
I took them at their word. It's been a long year
of blood moons and mixology. Towels in the bass drum,
handkerchiefed high hats. I've lost track
of how far I've driven straight—if the world is round, I may
have ripped right through. You can't write through an absence,
you only end up giving form to silhouette. But what's wrong
with being the butcher, anyway? Every town needs one.
Say there's been a deluge of roadkill and the meat

is going to fester and boil. I had the idea
that any good story needs an ending worthy of the sum
of its miseries, but I can't plot my way out of this one,
Lily, I can't even put on my fucking shirt. I'm sorry
I dragged you back into all this. I'm sorry I made you watch.
If it makes you feel better, I'll be the butcher—
seems fitting, all this smoky blood, these ligaments
forming lines. I found Jakov against our palm tree in the front
with a knife, and I took the knife away, so then it was mine.
Couldn't find the words to explain that he had it wrong,
you don't need a blade to take off your hands,
you just need a pen and a heart full of townsfolk,
starving, neglecting their herds because they can't
get out of bed, watching the last heifer rot in the sun,
because the butcher's gone missing, he's lost
in the terminal, making eyes at friends
who are not friends, a whole lot of harmonicas,
and the thing about the gas station
is the pumps are still on, sour green blinks
wandering the night, but nobody has the guts
to cross the yellow line. I had the idea
I could drink my way back into our bedroom,
that same sagging mattress, our clothes scattered like snow,
like fingertips in a freezer left open
in case the butcher comes back.

# II.

# Elegy

We were the ones slow-dancing with streetlamps, fashioning gallows out of bottle and bone, we were singing from the tops of pines, the birds didn't know what to make of us and our scramble toward the sky, we were building walls in the backyard and knocking them down the next morning, on the metro we were always swimming in pools of our own sweat, on midnight treks for smokes we caught rain on our tongues and carried it back home, we were cages of light barreling into the gutter, the only place we fit, our mating calls resembled quarters in a blender, our path was marked by the string of baffled dog catchers and gas station receipts, the candy in the freezer was not candy, the burns down our arms were not from the stove, the 40s in the recycling were stained with lipstick and piss, we were pipes bare save for resin, we were busted chainsaws, fences full of holes, we were the mad ones, our pockets full of rattlesnakes, our mouths full of cement, our pals were the garbage men and ghosts, we were the haloes around headlights when the sky cried mist, we were white-knuckling on the freeway while earthquakes shook the streets, we were twilight cathedrals crumbling and cold, we were weeping on the pavement when the blackout let us go.

# 4AM, TUESDAY

At 4am, the only commercials are for call girls,
penile stimulants, animal rights campaigns.
An occasional Discovery Channel documentary. Maybe a sitcom.
So many people tossing their remotes and touching themselves,
on sofas and shag carpets across the slow blue land,
disregarding their open curtains
and piles of unwashed clothes. This is all to say
there's a lot of sadness in TV dinners
and drinks left out overnight, long enough for moths
to get curious, drown and get tossed.
I feel like that octopus
who figured out how to open a jar underwater
from the inside, and instead of swimming out,
just sat there, sort of looking around.

# MIGRATION

You put a thousand birds in a tree and make them sing,
and it sounds like water. You put a thousand birds in a tree,
and then you put a bullet in one, and the rest
take flight. You take a coffee pot
and make it gargle steam, and it's your best friend
drunk in a hotel room, alone, somewhere on the Strip,
but you know nobody can hear your friend, so you plug your ears
until the coffee's done. You take a book of matches
and light it up outside the pharmacy. You take your pills,
wash them down with whatever she left you:
maple syrup, hard root beer. Easy. You take a man
with ragged nails and tell him, *This is your*
*hotel room. This mini-fridge? Your realm.* You take attendance
on your ventricles and find some lack of rhythm,
search bars and bookshops, the gym's lost and found.
You take a thousand birds and make them stop
flying south, you tell them you have all their old mates
at gunpoint. *No sudden moves.* You take a break
from eulogizing the living and remember you've got
coffee in the kitchen. You take a bowl of coffee grains
and leave it on the counter to absorb her lingering scent.
You take your sheets and wash them
along with your best friend's Marlboro coat. You take a body
of water and tell it to become a bunch of birds, but it won't,
it won't even look you in the eye. You take a thousand birds
and firebomb their tree—there, that silence
is the sound you've craved. Now relax. You take a piano
that's been drinking, a really sleepy man, you take a bullet
in a hotel parking lot and you put it back where it belongs.

# TRIGGER WARNING

Here is something that is true: at some point in broad nightlight,
you'll shave your pubes before going to a party
and end up ladling in a soup kitchen instead.
One time on Western and Expo,
a guy hyped on PCP charged a cop car naked,
like maybe if he smashed the dash hard enough
he'd break the windshield and not his hands, but he was wrong,
and we watched him hit the pavement and sob.
He was Tank Man in South Central, but the cops didn't care,
and neither did we, really, since we just blinked and walked away.
Another time I stopped outside a sorority house
because a girl was at her window; it was dark, she was applying makeup
violently, which I hadn't thought possible, and I don't think she saw me,
but I waved just in case. My friend Shane
said smoking helps you hike at high altitudes because your body
learns to deal with less oxygen, so maybe if I lock myself
in a hot-boxed closet, I'll figure out how to navigate my sex life
without smothering in the sheets. Here's a weird one:
I punch myself when I'm anxious and nobody's looking
just to take my mind someplace else, and I must confess,
it works. I don't know what the deal is with all these
hollowed out phone booths, but they give me the creeps,
and it's not like I have anything new to say about God or sex,
but I'm still talking. I've learned that if you want to be left alone in public,
you just have to curse in creative ways, like *fuckshitfuck!*,
and wear moth-eaten clothes, but if you end up in the wrong neighborhood,
lonely strangers will stick to you like glaze—like last Friday
when I found myself handing a smoke to a bald gangbanger
who gave me girl advice for a good twenty minutes
at MacArthur Park. Most of it was him complaining
about his ex and hair loss, but the dude meant well.

I wish I knew what to say about gin stagger and needles,
or how to forget the press of open lips, but I don't.
My sermon is Zippo tricks and love notes on napkins,
my friends are my bruises, and I know I taste like nicotine,
but everybody tastes like something.
There was one time on Western and Expo when a man got really
      scared,
and rather than let anyone notice, he shattered his fists
against a checkered dash. Later, I saw a girl assault her own face
for some defect only she could see,
and then along the lake known for body bags and ducks, I shared a
      cig
with a guy about as lonely as me. Here's the truth: at some point
      everything ends,
and the streetlights turn off, usually because it's bright enough to see.

# STILL LIFE OF LILY

And there was love in the lip balm, and the feathers,
and the waist-length hairs you left draped across my pillow,
those power lines downed by a tree. And I said terrible sad things
to you while you were asleep, and I repeated them later on
to the bathroom mirror, after you'd brushed your teeth
and gone. And there was love in the flasks of Fireball,
and in the toilet bowl's warmth after you'd left it,
love in the ants out back, dragging stray pieces of glass
away from their hills, so tenderly—I took notes on their movements,
wishing I could touch you the same way. And you said
you'd never cried in your life, the morning after you sobbed
and stained my mattress, the morning after
I said terrible sad things to you, believing you were asleep.
And I fell into other women's beds, and I swallowed
their perfumes, but despite my best efforts, they all tasted
like you. And I drank myself into the hospital. And you smoked
enough weed to kill a bull. And I scooped up all the remnants
and stray pieces of glass and built this bouquet of words
that will never be enough. And I tried again.

# HEIRLOOM

Finally it's middle night, the town's asleep
and I can watch my breath hit the porch
without fear of friendly small talk
from golfers whose balls crossed the fence.
My father sings and strums throughout the day—
lovelorn ballads about winter following spring.
His voice cracks and twangs, he falls deep
into his Valley accent only then, when he thinks
I can't hear through the door. I truly am
my father's son, burying love notes
in our overgrown heirloom tomatoes,
giving the dirt her words. This late at night,
he's due to come down in his underwear,
use the bathroom, drink
from the tap, and in that moment, we'll be
the only ones awake in this single-stoplight town.
*Goodnight, Dad. Goodnight, son.* From my father, I got
my fingernails, my slouch, my rearview mirror.
From somewhere I'm not sure of, I got these lungs
full of confetti and a case of sleeptalk
only she could stand. Here in Shenandoah,
where no one but family knows my name,
I can watch frost creep over the garden and listen
to my father toss and turn upstairs, shaking
the house with every stir. If he talks in his sleep,
I can't hear him through the door.
One of us will have to die first.

# Exile / Homecoming

Sitting on an Arizona gravel lawn half-past eleven,
I thought about where it all came from: one big rock
shattered and tossed across a thousand yards.
And then I wondered if I was sitting on one big rock
or a thousand small ones. Or how when I take a drag
off my cigarette, I'm really inhaling dozens
of burning plants, that were maybe lined in a row,
maybe not. When does paper stop being a tree,
when do I stop being the one writing this poem?
*Jackson, come home*, Lily said. *Jackson, please.*
That's what I used to say to myself whenever I stepped
out of my body and wouldn't step back in. Van Gogh
sent his lover a part of his ear. Was that his best attempt
at coming home? If he'd sent his hand or his head,
would that have been closer? The gravel is gravel
because it's no longer a boulder, the tobacco stops
being a plant once it's rolled, but how many appendages
do I have to lose before I stop being me?
*Jackson, come home. Jackson, we're tired. Jackson,*
*I hate you, I love you, Jackson, I can't tell the difference.*

# No More Rain, No More Roses

I kick the dog in my dream and wake up
to no dog. I carve my initials
in an old dead tree, and though the tree
is wreathed in leaves, the leaves
are really toilet paper. The ice
throws me down the hill
outside my apartment, to the bottom
of another hill, one with grass
that won't freeze sheet-solid.
Goddamn that drip won't go down
with the bourbon or smog—my friend says
she's got a bobcat in her head,
but she won't let me near him,
she's going to wait it out in the tub.
My brother says he's determined
how exactly the world is flat,
there are no hills to get thrown down.
My ex-lover says nothing, nothing
at all. I soak my feet in turpentine
and leave tracks for no one to follow.
I toss a chair through a window, stomp
on orange plastic bottles, make a scene.
This barista winks as she passes me
my fishbowl mug. I fry my eggs
in bacon grease, drive in circles
around the hill. I know
there's love somehow draped
in all this toilet paper, its cursive sprawl,
there's always love, it never
really stops, does it?

# CURBSIDE DIRGE

How sweet it is to drink too much coffee
under the manic flatness of streetlamps
while cars fly by and police choppers shush
overhead. I wonder if it matters
who's on the pill, or who's taking Prozac
because they can't stop staring at bridges.
Last night I slept in the library, watching
drunk students wander the quad,
laughing, tripping on boards and empty cans.
I wanted to hear what they were saying. I wanted
to follow them home and listen as they called
exes and slurred pleas for them to come over,
maybe catching dial tones, maybe having clumsy sex
they wouldn't remember.
Sometimes I think we're kidding ourselves when we say
we know what we want, or whom we'd like to fuck,
how many times we've been talked down
from rooftops. How lonely are the freeways,
where everyone's in sight but out of touch.
How strange to see friends with razor skids
and burns down their thighs. It doesn't matter.
I can fall in love on the metro or on the moon,
and I'll just end up on this same dusty corner, blowing smoke
on strangers as they walk and keep walking away.

# Madness

They gave me fancy words and pills that stuck like Velcro in the throat // I signed a contract promising to follow my friend down the well // When the lights went out at Wal-Mart, for a moment we were not all hideous, and then we were // My brother let them take a peek inside his ribs when I lacked the resolve // In a vacuum, sound swallows itself, vibration succumbs to stasis, because you can't drown in nothing // You can only fight release // When I really lose my mind, I hope someone tells me, but I didn't when Jakov started seeing cameras hidden in streetlamps, diamonds down the well // I didn't tell him // Just handed him another beer

# DANDRUFF

falling into my date's drink and she's not noticing,
too busy seeking eye contact, pushing
back her hair with painted nails.
She takes a sip, and as scalp tumbles down her throat,
I feel my bones sing. There's something electric
about disappearing into another body,
like the teeth that rake your hand as you thrust it
into snow, or jolting awake after another
fifty-story fall. At the party, girls were spinning
like tops as guys poured shots
over their heads. I wanted to be
the alcohol, descending gracefully until
it settled beneath crazed heels. I wanted to be
anyone else, there in the lungs of it,
every footfall a reminder of where I'd been,
every crack in my voice an echo of someone
I'd once heard, but the jukebox halted, signaling
it was time to go, gather our belongings,
beg someone to take us home. The train
sobbed in the distance, and a girl said,
*Shut up already*, tossing her bottle in that direction,
turning before the glass scattered like rats.

# CROON

There are no explosions here, no friends
checking into psych wards, no cocaine
on fingertips or lodged in ATMs—
here it's all birdsong and chamomile
by the fire, but Goddamn it I miss you
and your conspiracy theories twelve shots deep,
the hymns we crooned over the LA sky
as our eyes filled with tears over spilled mixers
or unanswered texts. We were constantly
on the brink of something unruly, a freezer
packed with acid candy, an empty topless bar,
nothing made sense on our perpetual trip drifting
up dry riverbeds. These days I can't buy
a pack of smokes without beating it
against my palm, the way you used to on Fig,
up those blurry alleys, in those headlights
we will never see again. You and me, we're limping
out of that blackout into rooms of phony smiles,
hand sanitizer, double Windsor knots, and though
I took that flight and left you passed out
in the garage, I was there when the roof
fell through beneath our feet. I am still there now.

# PAST LIVES

That's right, I was a gum stain on Sunset, I was the tongue that spat it out. I was a tear in a speaker buzzing like a fuse. Everyone shut up. I was channel surfing in Big Bear when my friend jumped out of a tree. When all the students swarmed the bars, I was an expired condom in a wallet, but I was also the wrapper, and the wallet. Listen: I was a June bug seducing a floodlight until the morning smacked me down. I was a bouquet of daffodils tossed off the bridge. I was thinking about how many of my friends are dead, or how I would even know. I was watching videos of people putting their clothes back on after sex. I was the clothes and the skin they concealed. I remember now: I was a television in an empty room, I was a mirror marred with lipstick, I was a squirrel stuck in hot tar.

# SHANE

College kids are keying car doors
down Clinton—the bars are closing. I find Shane
shambling down an alley with bits of twig
in his hair and beard. His hands keep working
the dark like dough and he won't meet
my eye. A grieving father is allowed to curse
at corner store clerks and smash glass
against cool brick, pass a bagged bottle back
without wiping his spittle from the lip,
stumble home to his rag-draped bench
and weep. A grave is the earth's perverted
laying on of hands. A pack of stolen cigarettes
shared beneath smog just might be
enough to stave off thoughts of death. At least
that's what I tell myself as Shane sobs,
tells me yet again how he got that titanium
in his wrist, snarls at a couple fraternity brothers,
extends his claw of a hand, which I take,
feeling his knuckles crumble in my palm,
and like that the two of us bear witness
to the gloom of faces wreathed in steam,
pavement warped by heels, ghosts
who weave cursive in the worried space between.

# Dogs

*after Sarah Carson*

Good lord how those dogs howled
through the chain links, my blood
on their lips, good lord the screen,
the screen we punched out to feed
smoke to the inky night, good lord
the spliffs, good lord the lungs
on those dogs and our staggerstep
waltzes through summer sweat,
good lord opening my eyes to you
in the morning, slipping into a pair
of my boxers, sipping flat
champagne, good lord the avocados,
the avocados atop burnt toast
in the dawn's cinnamon light,
your tongue against my shoulder,
your fingers in my hair, good lord
the guitar, how it looked in the gutter,
good lord your necklace you forgot
again and again, hanging
on my corkboard, your scent settling
in my sheets, these sheets I cradle
moving slow through dreamy space,
good lord the night we came
home to my room packed
in boxes and bags, how we held
each other like matches in a book,
good lord how you hurt me
in that driveway in the rain,
the sirens, the stares, good lord
we cannot be the only ones

who ignore stars in favor of dark,
who pluck strings like gray hairs
and shred letters only to tape
them back together, good lord
those dogs, what they were trying
to tell us, what we wouldn't hear.

# EVERYTHING BROKEN IS
# BEAUTIFUL, YOU IDIOTS!

I came back to Los Angeles
with a pocket full of photos and a pocket full of glass,
eyes brimming with ginger ale I'd hoped would mix well
with whatever my friends were drinking these days,
but I was not prepared for these tabletops
and pocketknife lines, the hell they hock up
when 6am is time for another bump. And that's all
to say nothing of the sledgehammers, the crowbars
and tall cranes, grave robbers ripping through
our old study spot, the Denny's where Rockwell
puked in the sink, the field where Lily and I
discovered our monopoly on sunlight—
now the hedges are trimmed below eye height,
the windows overlook pristine cement, and all my friends
left for Echo Park to try and be somebody.
I don't want to be somebody. I know I'm only as tall
and strong as a cornstalk, and that's fine by me
as long as I end up a part of a row. But I'm still stuck
on the bitter throat drip and rolled up bills, Youssef's sad look
when he called us walking clichés, and that stench clinging
to my jeans even now, three days after that skunk
sent me and Skyler pounding dirt, the fists put through walls,
my achy jaw, our laughter, naked outside Dodger Stadium,
the chemical bath and dog hair, vows sealed in smoke
but forgotten come morning, and who will save us
from the great gray blank? Who's going to re-set
the bones in our arms, dust us off, put us down
in beds that aren't chainlinked or hooked to IVs
in the hospital I swore I'd never see again?
For the moment, everyone's heart's still going and the sky

hasn't become a pair of arms, but I'm too scared
of ambulance lights to breathe—we're empty windowpanes,
gnarled up knuckle hugs, I've become everything
we once swore against, and all my friends
just keep slicing straws, they're going to be somebody
better than whoever they left back on 29th,
they're going to trade any semblance of stability
for buckets of snow and salt, and here I am,
broke and out of breath, shambling after pleasure zealots
who have long since stopped looking back.

# III.

# ATROPHY

More and more, I feel like the bits of tire left
in skid marks on the freeway where people crashed
and likely died. Or the blood I rub off
my fingertips as I crush this mosquito
on my thigh. More than anything, I feel like
a bathroom trash bin full of fingernail clippings,
or the clippings themselves. If dust really is
mostly skin particles, I wonder how much of you
is left in our old room, on the now empty
bookshelves and floors. I know you feel the same:
like no one will ever notice the flakes of your lip
left on theirs, the eyelashes you leave in their suitcases,
the echo like tinnitus every time they hear your name.

# CHOKE AND SIGH

July heat has got me weeping at the bus stop,
clutching old letters and crossing out words
until it's nonsense: *I gentle sex cold. Now unbearable heal hair.*
Sitting here on Sunset, feeling my lungs light up and fry,
I toss away my filter, lick my lips in the sun. I keep thinking about
    the night
I fell down the courtyard stairs—how the wine between my teeth
probably looked like blood, how the partiers
just kept partying. I found some bananas in the pantry
and laid the peels out where people were dancing, but nobody slipped.
A couple nights later, I tried to make love to a woman, but I kept
    laugh-crying
so I zipped up her pants and went home. It wasn't fair,
and I have yet to call and explain what happened—how I wandered
    up 30th
past chalk-stained fences with my hands
splayed out like wings. It's all fucked, this city
and these lights and this noise. It's all a bunch
of pseudo-intellectuals and kids huffing paint.
The freeways are choked with wrecked frames
of metal and bone, and the drivers just keep driving.
On the bus I sit and watch a boy braid his sister's hair.
He's got his eyes screwed up, his lips parsed and tense.
The boy looks at me and grins.
His sister says, *Don't stop,* and our bus rocks along
to a backdrop of exhaust, punching holes in the air we all breathe.

# BIRD

We're spitting lies in kids' faces, dropping
barrels off bridges, kissing our fists
as we throw them into trash compactors, gods
of our own lives. Take-out Thai and wine coolers
in our bathrobes, ink exposing all
our hidden parts. On my balcony,
a dove has made her nest and she won't move—
I think she's scared I'll take her eggs and swallow them,
but we have an understanding: I won't hurt her
if she won't tell my roommates I cry in my underwear
while our neighbors roam drunk in the courtyard
every night. I don't hurl bricks or chairs
like they do, not anymore, so I'm glad she chose
my balcony and not one of theirs. I feel no need
to scoop her up, twist her neck
and scramble her eggs for the girl I left
on my pillow, because there is no girl,
no scribbled note or panties on the floor. So that's
where we are, watching strangers kiss in the rain, performing
oral sex on our coffee mugs and leaving them
out to dry. It's a careful lonely we drink when the sky
is full of propellers and wings, or hollow points
marking God's awful spot in the clouds.

# APOCALYPSE

This is my hand, this is my fist, this is the sound
it makes against cartilage, on the staircase or
in the chapel, and this is the way it cradles air
it's too scared to release. So what do we do now
that the foundations of our homes have splintered
and the unions are on strike? How can we go on
when we keep texting our loan officers
in our sleep? I'm telling you now that this
is probably the end, soon the sky will fall
like a sheet of glass, the sea will boil away.
This is my hand, this is my pen, this is my poem
about the apocalypse and how maybe
it's already happened. This is the stale gray of the ER
and the parade of pills down my throat.
This is my therapist, her cute dimples,
her wedding ring. These are mud dauber wasps
paralyzing spiders, stacking them dozens deep
for their larvae to eat once they hatch.
These are thin spider legs folded like Kleenex, in neat
little piles, and that's us, in our houses and cubicles,
in our relationships and paper skulls.
This is depression, this is a prescription, this
is the realization that the world will be just fine
without me. This is desperation. This is a love note.
These are my lips. Those are yours.

# NOVOCAIN

I'm back from the dentist and the bottom half of my face
is just rubber stapled down—fleshy pulp that moves
but doesn't feel. When I speak, I'm a four-year-old,
and the drive home was terrifying—not the thought
of a crash, but the thought of trying to explain myself
in blabber speech to an amused cop, or praying
over a dying stranger, making her leave this world
to a soundtrack of, *I'm so sowwy*, on repeat. I'm confident
I could bite off my lower lip, but I'm not brave enough to try.
I don't know what I'd do with it, anyway: put it in ice water
and drive to the ER, or just sit and hold it for a while?
The upside is that, for once, I can feel how my face feels
to others: the slant of my jaw, the push of my tongue
against my own arm. That must be how it felt for you.
I know now how your fingers cruised through my beard,
over my chapped lips. I wanted to call you up and tell you,
but forgive me, Lily, I sat down and wrote this instead.

# American Spirits

And the worst part was she'd only had a bottle and a half,
which isn't much for her, and I shredded my soles running,
just to find her slumped on the porch with a pack
of American Spirits on hand. She cried out
all the alcohol and told me about her mother, how to mix
a French 75. I pitched a dozen Valium across the lawn
to make the cats feel a little less empty, a little
less like spiders stuck in Coke bottles.
We ordered gin and tonics at Denny's
and snorted orange juice onto the rug. I know another girl
who is sad all the time, who smokes weed
and used to slip her hand into mine
on walks through golden hour haze. When I left her,
she talked about barbiturates like old friends and gave me
a fistful of well-conditioned hair. She once said, *I'll kill you,*
*I'll fucking kill you, I love you so much*, in plumes
of pillow and breeze. Now it's the three of us on our own,
balking at prescription pads and chain-smoking
outside parties, spitting in gutters
to keep the currents strong. It's winter in Los Angeles
and the trees keep tearing up the sidewalks. People notice
when you've been crying, but they rarely mention it,
and hordes of feral cats flood roadways, saying, *Hit me,*
*don't hit me, please hit me, do it now.* There are times
when the world feels like a wound
no amount of pressure can seal.
We're disillusion manifold, mounds
of flaming tires, and our friends worry because
we haven't been smiling or answering their calls, and they're right,
something is wrong, but we'll be the first to admit. It's 1am—
tonight I'm alone in the Culver City Denny's, wiping orange juice

out of the carpet and setting every other smoke aside.
I am not holy. I hold my vices like a crutch.
I'm still stuffing my backpack with pipe bombs,
still helping loved ones look for graves.

# Salton Sea

Past the road's end, past the car hulls and dormant
oil rigs, past the outhouses leaking graffiti, there
is a beach made of bones, dry vertebrae, split ribs,
jaws and teeth, and past that is an acid sea, the bones float
when tossed like bread, nothing lives, past the sea
is vast nothing, desert like an ice rink, like flesh
when a bandage is stripped, and past that,
mountains chew the sky, windmills creak lullabies,
and someone must be up there watching this rubble of days,
someone must be laughing at how sad it all is, they must.

# Mirror Test / Photographs

Here's the trash can we filled with hydrogen peroxide,
here's the skunk that ruined my jeans. Here's the knife
Christian kept waving around, the nick he took out of
my thumb three days before he lost himself, when we
were still giggly, margarita mad. Here's the bobby pin
I keep in my wallet, though Lily probably doesn't wear
bobby pins anymore. Here's the way I rub my eyes
mid-panic attack, and here's the look I get from friends
who don't know me well enough to ask what's wrong.
Here's the tremor I catch in the diner next to
this old man whose hands somehow shake more
gracefully than mine. Here's the hotel where Jakov
lost himself in laced coke and conspiracies,
thrown playoff games, Pepe Silvia. Here are bad
first dates in rotating dive bars because
I can't remember how to small talk for shit.
Here are the months flattened by booze
when I still believed hope was the thing with teeth
you keep locked in the medicine cabinet. Here are the days
I broke things just to revel in my inability to put them
back together, like bones, like people, because I lost myself
for a minute there, I threw out my back just for a glance
at my reflection, I've got to find me somewhere in this
blacktop cacophony, I guess I don't love you anymore.

# THE CONSOLIDATION OF LONELINESS

One night in West Virginia, in a cabin in a blizzard
in a town of six hundred, I sat in bed alone
and listened to my neighbors having sex.
It was desperate and raw and I couldn't bury my head
deep enough to drown it out. The pillows were cinderblocks
and the floor was the keel of a ship
rocking underfoot with waves of fuck.
I knew it was time for me to leave, time
to lace my boots and step outside,
to write goodbyes on the windows of every shop
with my tongue, so I did, and when I reached the place
where the road met the river, I threw rocks
and watched them flit across the ice. Dawn crept out
like fingers collecting the sky
and I wiped my hands in the snow. I didn't cry,
I didn't follow my tracks backward into the cabin
like a man looking for his keys at the bar.
Instead, I found a well-lit bench
and waited for someone to pass.

# A CLEAN HEAL

I'm sorry boys, I lost my head—stumbled over
one too many turnstiles, barked my knuckles past
clean heal. The last time I said anything true
was in an Albuquerque Super 8, and the only person
listening was getting paid to check me in. And yes,
I caught those planes, flushed those drugs, listened for the howl
of hunted things we once threw down Sunset, but heard nothing.
Incredible, two years of exile and I'm still an asshole.
I expected to glean some sagely wisdom
from the rest stops and ferries, pool halls and drive-throughs,
but here I am, prowling these same streets, wondering
who's going to take me to bed. Fucks me up pretty good,
knowing there's no one new to ruin. I have no name
for the sound a cigarette makes when it flares the ends
of your hair, but the sound I make when I think of friends
and bathtubs is somewhere mid-sigh and sob.
I'm still getting used to the jawscape of a city
without someone to hand me gauze. I talk and talk
about starting fresh, but we all know the jig is up.
Time's a hot bullet. We keep our photos in frames.

# ESSAY ON TORNADOES

There's a dip in the road outside my apartment.
I like to sit and watch cars' undersides get gutted,
because if you don't know to slow down,
you always scrape out. It's not the road that does
the damage, though—it's the driver hitting the gas.
Leaning into the violence: that's where the hurt
finds form. Drunk drivers survive their crashes
because their bodies don't fight back. I read
about a man who got sucked into a tornado
and lived because a slab of concrete knocked him
unconscious straightaway. His body didn't fight,
just rolled with the wind. My buddy Youssef told me
proper tornado defense is getting in the tub
and laying your mattress overhead.
His friend did that in Tuscaloosa and survived
when the storm took everything away.
She said it struck with perfect whimsy:
one kitchen cabinet gutted, the other left untouched,
all its bowls and wine glasses pristine. When I first came to
this place, I thought there was a beauty in resistance, that
accepting the blows signified some weakness,
some lack of resolve. So I looked at photographs,
carried mementos, imagined my ex-lover's face
in place of strangers' and friends'.
I drank to remember and drank to forget.
Found myself blackout in the alley behind Mercy
with her name sliced into my palm. Listen when I tell you
something I needed to be told: there is nothing beautiful
about surviving the end times and watching highlight reels
to reminisce. God's the saddest guy in the bar because
he remembers what every key on his chain

has locked. Last week I spun out on I-80 mid-storm
and waited for the glass to shred my cheek.
I don't know why the semis spared me—
I'd cranked the wheel left like a dumbass. Evidently
I haven't learned anything at all. It is work
to carry a head full of maggots and not feed them
table scraps, to think of the one you love
loving someone else and not kick the gas pedal
straight into a storm. I am trying my best here to say
something that is true, but Christ almighty,
these fucking photographs, the gears that gut my heart.

# Blood Moon

Barefoot on the blacktop, pen in hand, I don't care
about the way the moon is wreathed in red gas
or how the clouds avoid it—I'm here watching
only in hopes that you are too, on the quad
or on your roof, 1800 miles away, or just a phone call.
But no, I know you're out here as well,
and hearing each other's disembodied voice
might make sorrow rise from this hum
into a scream—it might remind us that we're each
walking and breathing, living without the other.
I hate that we can do that. Here in the heavy dark,
I'm listening to cicadas call to their mates,
God knows how far away. I'm wishing
I could call out loud enough for you to hear,
that maybe my voice could ricochet off the moon,
that red mirror of us all, and land at your feet, calm
and self-assured, but no, there's no use pretending.
I am not strong enough to do something like that.

# OUTSIDE

I keep finding myself loitering in the snow, watching strangers clink their beer steins through the pane. In my Iowa apartment, I am always scrolling through photos of friends in far places, remembering their tics, their catchphrases and perfumes. The song of skin on skin is always spliced with cold static. My tongue is too scared to speak. I lie in my driveway and watch jets saunter by and wonder if the woman I love is inside, sipping a Coke, adjusting her seat. I want to know why my voicemail won't stop coughing, why my bruises look like smiles. The graveyard is a nightclub, when viewed in the right light. A body is a bullet hole that can't be filled or sealed. Falling is a state of being. I am trying to break the glass.

# HOTEL (SINT MAARTEN)

The German dancer at the booth to my right
was flashing sexy eyes my way, not seeing the tranquilizers
in my smile, and I wanted so badly
to take her back to my hotel room,
but instead I choked on my salad
and left alone. It's strange fighting insomnia
on a comforter so clearly intended for sex—
honeymoon sex, affair sex, desperate marriage-saving sex—
and relying on my mini-fridge and shower cap
for company. On the way back,
I passed six strip clubs and a sex shop,
and I didn't know what to say, or whom to say it to,
so I said nothing. Now I'm on the roof,
wringing my hands and watching a pair of flashlights
meander down the dock, one intrepid, the other hesitant,
both burning with the desire to be doused.
What is this loneliness from foreign cocktails
and hotel lights on the bay, or pop-ups
advertising sexy singles in my area?
These predictable erections and furtive looks—
all the little people drifting out alone
with the wind and the water, the lime rinds and salt,
while cover bands blare anthems to crowds
immersed in their meals. In the restaurant,
there was a bathtub full of lobsters. Their claws
had been torn off, so when the waiter came to grab them,
they couldn't put up a fight.

# WAITING ROOM

Around the time my girlfriend
started sobbing in her sleep,
my roommate downed two dozen Valium
and punched a hole in the drywall
over her desk. The ER is cold
even without the air conditioning on,
walking past burn victims and epileptics,
straining to stare ahead at pastel morale posters.
*From 1-10, how badly does it hurt*
*today?* My girlfriend came over
and said her inability to cry
was her favorite thing about herself.
I laughed and bit my lip instead of hers.
My roommate came home from inpatient
and brought a new friend. Fall came
but the weather didn't change.
My therapist told me I was drinking
*problematically.* Questionnaires and pamphlets.
Vitamins and prescriptions. I cut off
all my hair and my therapist
didn't notice. *You look tired*,
she said. My girlfriend started bawling
every time we said goodnight. My roommate
stopped asking me for advice.
Winter came and people kept sunbathing.
My therapist said, *Are you currently drunk?*
I logged the pain in a legal pad daily
from 1-10. I watched the skyline
for a change. A year came and went.
My girlfriend left me. No, I left her.
No, she left me. No one died.

# IV.

# Visions of Lily

For example, her toes curled up in our cold bed,
her eyes like ashes, the goosebumps along the small
of her back, and I want to know if anyone else
has celebrated her earlobe the way it wants to be celebrated,
like a ten-liter bottle of champagne popped in a room
of only two, she said she liked my collarbone,
its twin birthmarks I call moles, she said anything
looks better in candlelight, even dead flowers, even
a glass of water, that's really a glass of vodka,
which is really an invitation for departure,
and maybe I lied when I said I was okay, maybe
I gathered all those handfuls of matches
and stuffed them in my mouth to replace
her name, memories of blowing smoke through open
windows, fumbling with condoms at dawn,
memories of all I can no longer remember, like
letters tossed bridgeside and immediately missed,
voices meandering airspace in waves no one
can pick up, she taught me to trace a shadow
and acknowledge its ends, she brought me avocados
and took the knives away, and maybe it was unfair of me
to hope I'd kiss the part in her hair again, unfair
to pray that I'd be the only one she took to bed,
but here, I've put the vodka down, I'm holding out
my arms like open drawers ready to be filled with anything,
anything at all, thumbtacks or blouseflow, roses, dirt,
I'll trust my tongue over a toaster, I am staying
very still here in my right place.

# VEINS / LETTERS / MERCY

No one has ever loved me like the phlebotomist.
He takes me by the elbow, cradles my wrist,
slips the needle in with practiced grace.
Tells me I make his job a breeze, *If
everyone had veins like these, God would be
too kind.* All I have to give is blood,
some change for Shane on his curb, mercy
for the bat I net on the stairs.
I have my grandfather's veins—bulgy,
desperate to meet the air. They congregate
and conspire. Cut my heart's supply, like dynamite
laced into railroad tracks. I have prayed
to pills and pilsners, the refuse of expired loves,
their marginalia, voicemails like tired ghosts.
Dear phlebotomist, I don't believe in your God.
I don't believe in your love either. I'm going
to pay someone to plug these veins with coiled steel,
cut the flow, scrawl a prescription for something,
I don't know, Vicodin, amnesia,
something merciful like that.

# On Nothing

I'm afraid there's no good way
to become dirt. You can choose
to carry a pistol or perfume
and the bus will still cost you
two twenty-five, the rain will still
fuck up your hair. Stranger,
I will be the bad thing
that happens to you, but if
not me, it'll be the man
fingering his pocket lint, the dog
gnawing its leash. Funny how
easily we chew and swallow food
while in some distant country
a kid's belly's a balloon.
You can empathize with servers
or the ants you find in the stall.
It's your call. Your fingers itching
to slide between cotton and skin—
whose, you're not sure, but there is
someone out there who's perfect
for you, and that someone is probably
dead. Nothing is something because
we've given it a name, the space we cut
between beds and bathrooms doesn't give
two shits how many words we know, and
please oh please let me come over tonight,
I promise I'll sleep on the floor.

# PARTY

That's me in the kitchen, falling
into the girl with platinum hair,
staring out the window at a mob
of bodies clad in sweat.
Music like sirens and clash,
liquor soaking plaid.
I am listening for your voice
through the white noise,
but you're not here—you're toasting
the new year back home,
held by handsome arms.
Throwing hands in dark alleys,
scrounging for spent butts, I knew my place,
I had my philosophies—the roaches
held up the sidewalks, the flasks
filled our coat sleeves—but now the clocks
have stopped singing,
the Valium's in the toilet.
Every morning I see you in my coffee,
billowing with the steam, and I pitch you
across the lawn. We're breaking up.
My cell phone keeps spewing four-letter words.
These days I do the Running Man on roofs
even the crows won't touch. I can't unpack
my mind without finding extension cords
and thighs. I'm throwing words
like hands, against walls now instead of flesh.
This is sleeptalk apocalypse, burning photos
in the sink, flashing strangers looks
like knives, but in an hour I'll be better,
I'll strip down and join the mob.

# ESSAY ON FACES

Mostly I think about faces—which kind
to make when the hero in the movie
slips on an avocado rind, how to wince
in a way that's equal parts pleasure and
please-don't-leave-me. Last call:
I hold a crowbar to the moon
to trace its careful seam. Bartenders
flash practiced grins, soliciting tips
from men with needle teeth. The animal
pummeling its fence as I meander up
58th shows me how to make my face
a meat grinder. When I was 23,
I contorted my face for 14 months
until permanent wrinkles made their home.
I entered the room where I'd first seen
my fingers disappear inside
another person's mouth and
hung my favorite mask over the door.
More stray dog stranded by rain, less
prodigal son popping champagne,
I aired out all my laundry and found
lipstick and sunglasses that weren't mine.

# DOVES AND SERPENTS

I spent a long time pretending:
that these fists weren't wrapped in cellophane,
that everyone knew my name.
On the bridge I watched a man
watch the river, but the river was ice,
and the man was a coat on the rail.
I've been thinking on the difference
between clutch and embrace,
how to hold a moth
without it drowning in dust.
Before I learned how to gracefully
disappear in a crowd,
I threw chairs to assert strength
over silence. I was always trying to leave.
I pity anyone who hasn't woken up
on a stranger's fire escape and gone back
to sleep. Lately the moon has been talking shit
to the snowfields, shadowboxing
just outside their reach.
Once I thought I could name
all the wasps in my brain,
give each one a bed and a bottle,
and then there were no wasps,
or else that's all there was:
one writhing ball of wings.
All this is to say
a long time ago I got lost—
I woke up on a stranger's fire escape,
but it was my fire escape,
and I convinced myself that words
could fill the space between things.

I was wrong. I was tasting saline
through an IV in the hospital
named Mercy when I decided
the moon throws sunlight back
like note-wrapped bricks,
steady hands make for shattered wrists,
we clutch because we care.

# LILY SAVES BEES

with soda when she finds them dying on the sidewalk,
sprinkling it like holy water on churchgoers' heads. I kill
black widows whenever I find them. I hope she'd understand.
The people we let ourselves love seep into us, like smoke into
car seats, Sharpie into skin. We pick up accents and gaits,
tremors and fears, stories we tell ourselves so many times
we come to believe they're ours. Lily doesn't wear makeup
but you wouldn't believe that if you saw her. She likes
daydreaming about Armageddon and how many people
are surfing or fucking or training service animals
right this second. I like feeding my veins toxins
and wondering where I am, how I got these papercuts,
how many flights of stairs I've tumbled down before
reaching this gray plain. When Lily strips and comes
into my arms, I hold her like a glass brim-full,
I repent to a God I hardly believe in,
and she doesn't understand.

# Escape Plan

Whenever I see a plane cruising overhead, I jump in
and imagine looking downward at my house,
where I'm going, where I've been, what I'm running from,
who's chasing me. It's usually someone whose tongue
I've bitten off, and they usually have needles,
knives, something sharp—never blunt, never as easy
and senseless as a mallet because that's not
how heartache works. I thought I was getting better
at amputations, but there's no such thing as a clean break
or a smooth getaway, which is why every attempt at escape
via flight ends in catastrophe: the man sitting next to you
has rabies, you fly into a cloud of ice,
your brain suddenly ingests itself, and still you try,
you practice pillow talk and sweet nothings, you go through
all the motions, knowing it will end, knowing someone
somewhere will have you placed on a bed of nails
and lay themselves on top of you, delicately,
stroking your face as they push and push.

# It's Snowing and I'm Lonely

And so with all that in mind, I'm thinking about
amateur porn stars and how often producers ask them
to recount how they lost their virginity right before
telling them to take off their clothes. And my friend
Margot, who was doing that for a while, who, after
I'd lifted her shirt, told me not to be afraid
to be rough as she lit a flowery candle. I'm looking now
at my stupid candy cane socks that found their way
to my feet because I was a quarter short for laundry.
I take my lithium pill, take another, consider a third,
feel silly as the snow glosses grass yards
outside. Little white pills, bigger than the ones
Christian stole from my bathroom the month he broke
down outside the film kids' party, cauliflowered
Shawn's ear. I'm considering how simple it would be
to turn on my phone and find someone to come over—
no cameras, just an apartment strewn
with leaves and tinfoil thatched to fabric,
static attraction, tea stains on my sheets,
all my best selves lost in the smattering haze,
and if I were to go looking for any one
through the blizzard, I'd lose my hands
in the little white pills, little white lies I tell
myself when the ceiling looks like skylight
yet the floor looks drowned in gore. I don't know
how to turn my heater on. Tonight I'm growing
icicles in my throat.

# Last Full Moon in Iowa

Sirens in the east, moving toward some tragedy, and
who would commit a murder under a moon like this?
Who would break anything, a window, a skull, knowing
she was watching from above? I have bronchitis
again—too many smokes and nights not knowing
how many rings you're wearing, whether
you remember my smell. Hours wheezing, wondering
what bad jokes I've been mumbling in my sleep.
Do dogs howl at the moon or to each other?
Did you know how much I love you is why
I wash my hands? Someday when I'm better,
I'll read you a list of the things you became to me:
runway, poltergeist, mourning dove, splint, in hopes
you'll kiss my sternum, crack the same ribs as before.

# BLACKOUT (MANHATTAN)

Head out the window of a rented car, swallowing sewer grate fumes, your blood's a scrambled alphabet of dark, you're passing bodies like blouses hung on hooks // Now a model is feeding you salt and pepper chips in a corner store, feel his fingers graze your tongue // You must have run away because this alley is empty and where are all your friends? // Fists high, you're yelling mania at the Google building as busloads of nonsense people point and laugh // Suddenly you're clutching receipts in a saloon plastered in porn clippings and Leather Girl beckons with a pitcher labeled Ass Juice and two glasses // You made it to the poetry reading and found your friends but Leather Girl has backed you into a corner, she's grinding you into stacked spines, and where did you go wrong? // Slouched in a subway station bench, Leather Girl's talking about the human condition and her words' blurred lurch has you eyeing the tracks // Someone tied a *Get Well Soon* balloon to a homeless man's arm in his gutter slump coma, was it you? // You notice you've lost your friends again, you're alone on the sidewalk with Leather Girl, mumbling to mask your slur, does she want to fuck you or rob you blind? // You don't want to die just yet, here in this crackling greenhouse, all these grinning strangers or friends, you can't tell // Breathless in the doorway of a bar full of pirates, you must have fled Leather Girl, did she chase you? // All the cars keep yelling your name // This ambulance won't stop following you around // Someone's address is scrawled across your arm // You can't make it out

# ABSENCE

When I think of you in the city,
sidestepping oil spots and
drunkards' catcalls, I want to burn
everything down—the supermarkets,
the frat houses, the cafés
serving kale. I see a woman
sipping kerosene and lighting
shake joints on the stove.
I see streetlights spreading tendrils
like box jellyfish. I'm trying
to explain the ghost limb you left me
but I don't know how. Let me try again:
when I think of you in the city
throwing back a screwdriver on the 81
I can't stop rubbing at my eyes
until they bruise.
Your bouncing, steady gait:
it's what takes you away, out of every memory,
toward a place where not everything is a tragedy
and I can't reach for your hand.

# SOMETHING BRAVER

I'm shadowboxing in my underwear.
The young deacon's got his face in a book.
The gangbanger's snapping rounds
out of a cold clip, and the widower's wincing
as he sprays perfume in the doorway
and tries to inhale the cloud.
We're all the same. It's a question of loss—
the hot tar night slipping in through our windows
and filling our lungs with the names of lovers
we've left crying on the steps, or pets
we've forgotten to feed—the friends we've lost
on our way to something braver.

# COLORBLIND

And red wine is cunnilingus and cobblestone,
titanium white is public massages,
black coffee is chain-smoking in Big Sur,
blue rags are knives at the bus stop.
Valium is eight dollars with a prescription,
like thirty-two gumballs or a movie ticket—
anything to drag me out of this house
where the walls peel like sunburn
and the floors are treacherous slick. I have blood
on my shirt from the fight I broke up last night
in the middle of a party, all of us feeling like flies
in the refrigerator. Green is my father's canoe
on the North Fork of the Shenandoah,
brown are my brother's eyes, the same
as my mother's, or those of the first girl
to sing me back to sleep. Reader,
sometimes I find myself in unfamiliar sun,
wondering what language I'm speaking, how
I ended up wearing this skin
and learned to believe in a mean God—
one who lets the rain fall like dimes off a high-rise.
Gray is my childhood home, or the diagnosis,
or the cure. White is a pile of collared shirts,
the books I buried in them. I know
I'm not supposed to scream and shout
when no one wants to move, but something cold
keeps pulling me towards the fray.
The palette is freezing. The technique is sound.

# CALL AND RESPONSE

When I tell my class to write a poem about nothing, I hope someone will turn in a blank page, but instead I get descriptions of empty beds, open mouths, the quiet between birdcall and response // I draw a hole on the blackboard, give my tired spiel about its ontology, the hole's reliance on dirt // Noon arrives // We all go home // My therapist tells me my face looks normal today // I say nothing's wrong // Two colonies of ants wage war over the crack beside my dumpster for three days before the rain sweeps them away // I dream of my ex-lover on another man's arm, and there's nothing I can give her, so I say nothing // Nothing pushes her away // A pink moon sings over cemetery crickets, and no one hears her, so she slinks back into the fog // Diesel runs in rainbows at the largest truck stop in the country, craving water it can repulse // I tell strangers in bars there's nothing sexy about desperate bravado, and I chomp ice cubes to prove my point // They laugh, leave // We all go home // At the end of everything, I'm a vestige making music out of nothing, and I know I look like an exit wound from where you stand now, but even silence makes a sort of sound // I worship nothing, gather it into my lungs // My fingers flee my hands // My heart is a photocopied fist // Photocopied laughter

# First Frost in Months

Here at the end of it all, lying naked next to
a woman I don't know, I am almost ready
to admit this was not a mistake,
I did not end up licking these lips
by some force of chance—
for the first time I am realizing
I may never breathe your coarse hair
in a room made roofless by smoke
again. I'm hoping you have weed
when you need it, a crying bench
for when you need to cry, a new set of arms
cool enough to soothe your ribs.
But here I am in bed. Someone's palm
brushes my chest and I taste my own tongue,
while someone's breath creeps into my ear,
punches the drum, kicks a beat.
How do I get back? Lily, I have to find me,
I don't know where I went. This chorus
of weepy soldiers, this grimace
holding my face in place against palms
pressing hard, too hard, but that's right,
I walked into this room
and closed the door. That was me.
That was our mistake, leaving
the barn door open to our goodbye.
I'm watching your nose scrunch up
in the memories I usually keep bundled
like sets of scalpels wrapped in felt,
hoping you're nestled in cashmere
with a bottle of cab, that you
finally fixed your janky-ass record player

and have someone who will nod off with you
to Frank Ocean. All evening I've been watching light
split shadows in quadrants dancing
up and down the walls. Manic spiders
seek shelter in their corners
and the faucet drips Morse code.
I keep waiting for someone to cut me
out of this photo, drop me in another one,
somewhere sunny, with windows
overlooking oceans that aren't corn.
I keep expecting to catch up to myself
and remember who left whom,
wringing my knuckles like thin throats.
I hope you do what you have to do
to fall asleep, that you've found a café
where no one knows your name,
why your eyes crinkle false when you smile.
I hope they serve their coffee strong,
give you a warm-up without you having to ask.
I can't rip you out of my mind like I wish
I could, I can't find you in anyone else's mouth,
oh sweet Jesus, Lily, your cold silhouette.

# LILY

# APOSTROPHE

I. Do you see what I'm seeing? The bricks are tumbling from cracked tar lots and the ground is drowning in white. Laughter escapes through barred windows into the night. Over the rooftops, lights flicker from the mountain's ribs—I wonder who is out there, whether they're wondering about me. In my dream we climb the temple and you shove me from the spire. Now I'm sprawled on the blacktop, pushing through sheets of memories like clothes on a line. The crows announce the evening, neon signs lure moths and men. With my knuckles raw and my cheek pressing concrete, I'm remembering the way my lips glowed when I last kissed you. I wish I could put you in that car, tie your hands to the wheel, make you look back as I did, because I did, and the sky didn't rain fire, the earth didn't melt. The sun whispered dirges too faint to make out and I slammed the gas into the floor. There's a cold wind tonight—do you see it? It's coming for us. It's scattering us like salt.

II. You are tearing holes in my pockets, spitting in my beer; now I have to blur you out of every film and frame. It snowed again and the blue fields glisten—leaves and lost hair dance across the sheen. I held out my hand all night like a net but caught nothing. In my dream you tip-toe in from Los Angeles with a shovel and a glass, the glass full of nothing—nothing you can cup in your palms, nothing that collects behind your eyes. Now I am collecting everything, all this ice beneath a salt sheet, warm oil rebuking the road. One time over a couple 40s, Shane told me I was a black hole, that I consumed everything within reach—he had half a beard and a bloodied eye. You and I both know a hole can't exist in a vacuum. It swallows to survive. Now I'm watching the tree line, just to see what weapons you'll have chosen when you finally descend. You've caught me in a blackout, here in this miraculous pile of nothing, this pit dug out of a pit.

III. This is something you can't have: in my dream your tongue is still in my cheek, your underwear in my hamper. From my basement apartment, I catch the cries of bedsprings upstairs. The snow abides, silencing the grass, but the moon's stagger through the steeples proves you're still out there, putting your coat on, licking a joint. Is it cold where you are? Are you alone? Lately I've been crawling the walls at parties, my only friend the slow clap of plates in the sink. Don't make me remember—now that I have no one to repeat my sleeptalk, I'm learning to do it myself. I thought I killed you in the rearview mirror, but somehow you keep finding your way back. In my dream my father reels in a smallmouth bass, jerking the hook deeper into its lip, waist-deep in green flow. He tells me, *Just don't hate her when she leaves.*

# A FAILED BALLAD

I'm on my back in the grass, watching jets slice the sky
like brushes on canvas, barbed wire on skin. Someone's singing
ballads across the park, but I can't make out all the words.
A cloud the size of Iowa City swallows up the planes,
and part of me wishes it would fall like a grand piano,
knocking us all deep into the earth. There are things I remember
and things I forget. I can't remember the last thing you said,
but it was probably something sweet, some inside joke neither of us
would find funny anymore. I remember the night we met, at a party—
I hit the lean hard and, stumbling home, tried to befriend
some dogs through a fence. They mauled my hand and my sheets
are still covered in blood. It won't wash out. It never does.
I guess the end of winter means the beginning of something new,
but everything is always happening, anyway, so here we are now,
sipping coffee in Founders Park, here we are lying in bed,
talking Neruda and doing our best Louis Armstrong impressions,
and here we are in ten years, trying hard to figure out
why we always reach through fences we know we shouldn't.
Last night I choked on lithium and watched a special about giraffes—
their goofy tongues, their necks they swing like clubs
when they fight. At the end of the show, a mother was defending
her child from a pride of lions, and she looked as if she might make it,
stomping a wall around the foal, but then she stomped him
in the head. She stood there and then looked downward, slowly,
to see what she had done. And then she ran, her pitiful skull
swinging on its bean pole, her voice silent because giraffes
are silent creatures. We are not silent creatures. I wish
I could sing ballads, but all I can muster are these lines,
these desperate slashes across paper, like vapor trails behind planes,
or the scars we leave on each other's hands every time we embrace.

# THINGS I'VE WANTED TO TELL YOU

I fought a dog on the corner of College and Dodge,
though maybe it wasn't a dog, maybe a deer
or a dove or a mirror. In this empty cathedral,
my friend and I carve lewd things into the pews
with bottle caps we've stashed beneath our tongues.
I find myself thinking of your elbows
and your chipped white nails, the sound
of the car door slamming between us.
The woman singing in the Chicago karaoke bar
had your accent, so I wanted to take her home,
drive my mouth into hers like a bus into a tree,
but my friend started bleeding from his knuckles—
I must have missed him punching the wall. Or maybe
it was me, I was bleeding, or the blood
was on my knuckles but belonged to my friend.
I know, they said the ice would hold,
I was fooled as bad as you. I know,
you kiss your pipe and pass smoke in figure eights,
while I choke on filters, blow through my nose.
My friend's father called again to inform him
that night was the night, no more chickening out—
*Don't you want to hear my last words?*
I've wanted to tell you everything,
how I burned my tongue on my coffee this morning,
how I wept for you on the roof, but I don't
want to explain. I watched a film
about men who love life-sized dolls,
anatomically correct sex toys they can cook for,
pretend to waltz with, photograph. You'd have loved it,
loved them, loved their model airplane obsessions,
loved the women who hurt them. You were always loving.

It was my favorite thing about you. All this time,
I've wanted to sing you lullabies about lilies and weed,
about names and the ways they blur and fray.
I wanted you to see me dancing
in someone's living room, alone,
all the party guests wary of the butcher knife
I kept waving, the lightbulb I'd fit
in my mouth. My friend caught me
mumbling in a concert crowd,
middle fingers to the ceiling in vain—
I'd seen ravens in the rafters.
He took me outside and his father called,
again. My friend didn't answer.
Eventually one learns to culture neglect,
to breathe in dark and exhale figure eights. Hello love.
It's been one year since I last heard your voice.
I want to tell you the truth: everything
reminds me of you, everyone talks Chicago,
the lilies are speckled with blood,
your blood, my blood, my friend's,
my friend said, *Tell me your last words,*
*I'll remind you in the morning.*

# NOTES

The final three lines of "Migration" borrow language from Tom Waits' "The Piano Has Been Drinking [Not Me]" and J.D. Salinger's "For Esmé—with Love and Squalor."

"No More Rain, No More Roses" borrows its title and the line, "I carve my initials in an old dead tree," from Tom Waits' "Walk Away."

The final line of "Heirloom" was inspired by Matthew Dickman's "Slow Dance."

"Croon" is for Jack Stulic.

"Apocalypse" borrows language from My Brightest Diamond's "This is My Hand."

"American Spirits" is for Sari Rachel Forshner.

"Mirror Test / Photographs" borrows language from Radiohead's "Karma Police" and repurposes the Emily Dickinson line, "'Hope' is the thing with feathers."

"Visions of Lily" borrows language from CocoRosie's "Animals."

"Doves and Serpents" borrows language from The National's "Secret Meeting" and EL VY's "No Time to Crank the Sun."

The final line of "Apostrophe" was inspired by Neutral Milk Hotel's "Two-Headed Boy Pt. 2."

# ACKNOWLEDGMENTS

Grateful acknowledgment is made to the editors of the following publications in which early versions of some of these poems appeared:

*Anklebiters Journal, The Boiler Journal, The Cincinnati Review, Colorado Review, The Des Moines Register, DISTRICT LIT, Gravel, Hobart, The Los Angeles Review, Menacing Hedge, Northern Light, Rattle, Rust + Moth, Sinking City, Verdad, Word Riot,* and *7x7.*

"Salton Sea" appeared as a broadside in the Mark Taper Hall of Humanities at the University of Southern California.

"Curbside Dirge," "The Consolidation of Loneliness," and "Choke and Sigh" were included in the chapbook *Pocket Full of Glass* (Tebot Bach, 2017).

Thank you to my instructors and mentors, without whose wisdom I would be lost: David St. John, Cecilia Woloch, Chris Freeman, James Kincaid, Molly Bendall, Mark Irwin, James Galvin, Josh Bell, and Elizabeth Willis.

Thank you to the University of Southern California, the Tin House Summer Writers' Workshop, and the Scottish Undergraduate International Summer School. Many thanks to the Iowa Writers' Workshop, as well (especially Lan Samantha Chang, Connie Brothers, Jan Zenisek, and Deb West).

My deepest thanks to Ruth Madievsky and Ryan Taylor for reading this manuscript (and earlier iterations) and providing invaluable feedback, friendship, and poems I hope mine someday match.

Thank you to my family for your constant support. I love you more than I can say.

I'm forever indebted to my friends who have put up with my nonsense, sustained me, and contributed to these poems, in subject matter or spirit: Vamsi Chunduru, Aaron Nelson, Jesse Noviello, Youssef Biaz, Skyler Garn, Blake Mason, Michael Matchen, Jean Frazier, Dave Fulmer, Emily Rawl, Katie Barreira, August Lührs, John Rockwell, Maria Rodriguez, Sari Rachel Forshner, Abdo John Hajj, Katherine Montgomery, Dalton Banh, Jordyn Avila, Jack Stulic, Marta Olson, Nate Fulmer, Daniel Fletcher, Josh Greenberger, Alex Haughton, Lisa Locascio, Samsun Knight, Tony Flesher, Zach Isom, Alex Moss, Jake Montgomery, Rob McFarland, Jamie Alliotts, Jordan Walker, and Zoe Citterman.

Thanks to the Write Bloody Publishing family for believing in this collection and bringing it into the world. Thank you, Zoe Norvell and Nona Leon, for designing the cover and interior, respectively. Finally, special thanks to my sister and editor, Katie Hogan.

# ABOUT THE AUTHOR

JACKSON BURGESS received his MFA from the Iowa Writers' Workshop and his BA from the University of Southern California. He is the author of the chapbook *Pocket Full of Glass* (Tebot Bach, 2017), and his poetry and fiction have appeared in *The Los Angeles Review, The Cincinnati Review, Rattle, Cimarron Review, Colorado Review,* and elsewhere. He lives in Los Angeles, CA, where he works as an editor and educator.

# IF YOU LIKE JACKSON BURGESS, JACKSON BURGESS LIKES...

*Born in the Year of the Butterfly Knife*
Derrick C. Brown

*Counting Descent*
Clint Smith

*Do Not Bring Him Water*
Caitlin Scarano

*Racing Hummingbirds*
Jeanann Verlee

*Stunt Water*
Buddy Wakefield

Write Bloody Publishing distributes and promotes great books of fiction, poetry and art every year. We are an independent press dedicated to quality literature and book design, with an office in Los Angeles, CA.

Our employees are authors and artists so we call ourselves a family. Our design team comes from all over America: modern painters, photographers and rock album designers create book covers we're proud to be judged by.

We publish and promote 8-12 tour-savvy authors per year. We are grass-roots, D.I.Y., bootstrap believers. Pull up a good book and join the family. Support independent authors, artists and presses.

**Want to know more about Write Bloody books, authors and events?**
**Join our maling list at**

# www.writebloody.com

WRITEBLOODY
QUALITY AMERICAN BOOKS

# WRITE BLOODY BOOKS